The Best Tales Ever Told
DRAGONS AND DEMONS

Written by **Stewart Ross**
Illustrated by **Francis Phillipps**

COPPER BEECH BOOKS
BROOKFIELD, CONNECTICUT

© Aladdin Books Ltd 1998
© Text: Stewart Ross/Aladdin Books Ltd 1998

Designed and produced by
Aladdin Books Ltd
28 Percy Street
London W1P 0LD

First published in
the United States in 1998 by
Copper Beech Books,
an imprint of
The Millbrook Press
2 Old New Milford Road
Brookfield, Connecticut 06804

Editor
Jim Pipe
Designed by
David West Children's Books
Designer
Simon Morse
Illustrated by
Francis Phillipps
Additional illustrations by
Ken Stott – B.L. Kearley

Printed in Belgium
Library of Congress
Cataloging-in-Publication Data
Ross, Stewart.
Dragons and Demons : myths of China,
Japan, and India / by Stewart Ross ;
illustrated by Francis Phillipps
p. cm. — (The best tales ever told)
Includes index.
Summary: A collection of twelve tales
drawn from the myths and legends
of Asia and the Far East.
ISBN 0-7613-0708-7 (lib. bdg.)
1. Mythology, Chinese—Juvenile
literature. 2. Mythology, Japanese—
Juvenile literature. 3. Mythology,
Indic—Juvenile literature.
[1. Mythology, Chinese. 2. Mythology,
Japanese. 3. Mythology, Indic.]
I. Phillipps, Francis, ill. II. Title.
III. Series.
BL1825.R64 1998   97-52575
398.2'095—dc21   CIP AC

CONTENTS

4 *The* MONKEY KING
Can a cheeky monkey become the Supreme Ruler of the Universe?

6 CHANG LUNG *the* DRAGON
Life is not always easy when you're a dragon in disguise.

8 *The* UGLY SCHOLAR
How horrible bullies turned a scholar into a fearsome demon hunter.

10 DANCING *out the* SUN
Can anyone tempt the Sun Goddess out of her cave?

12 *The* GENERAL *and the* BEES
Being nice to animals can have its rewards!

14 *The* WHITE SERPENT GOD
Will the wicked swordsmen get away with murder?

16 DREAMTIME
Travel back to a time when our first relatives lived under the ground.

18 *The* VOLCANO GODDESS
Life gets pretty hot when you fall in love with a volcano!

20 *The* DOLPHIN MOTHER
The story behind the sad cry of the dolphin.

22 RAMA *and* SITA
Can the handsome prince rescue his love from Ravana and his demons?

24 DEADLY RIVALRY
Who is the mystery warrior in a suit of golden armor?

26 *The* ELEPHANT GOD
What happens when dad cuts off your head?

28 TRICKY TERMS
29 WHO'S WHO
32 INDEX

INTRODUCTION

These twelve stories are some of the most famous ever to come out of Asia and the islands of the Pacific Ocean. They are drawn from many countries, including India, China, Japan, and Australia.

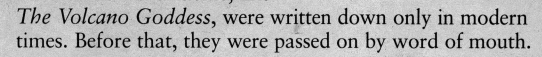

The Indian stories, such as *Rama and Sita*, are very old and are an important part of traditional Indian religion. Japan's *The General and the Bees*, on the other hand, is more recent – about 1,000 years old. The tales from the Pacific, like *The Volcano Goddess*, were written down only in modern times. Before that, they were passed on by word of mouth.

Myths, such as the story of *Chang Lung the Dragon* (*above right*), are entirely made up. Legends, such as *The White Serpent God*, are loosely based on events that really happened. Some of the images, shrines, and temples mentioned in these stories can still be seen today (*right*).

People told stories for many reasons. The best ones were not just entertainment – they tried to make sense of things readers and audiences didn't understand. *The Dreamtime* story, for example, was how the first Australians explained the beginning of life on Earth. *The Dolphin Mother* explained the sad noise that dolphins make. Storytellers often gave their tales a moral. This is a message about how people ought to behave.

Most of these stories have changed a lot over the centuries. To help you, we have picked out the best parts and made them easy to understand. We hope you'll enjoy them as much as those who first heard them many, many years ago.

A Guide to Tongue-Twisting
Some old names can be tricky to say. To make it easier for you, we have broken down long names into smaller parts.
For example, Surpanakha should be said "sir-<u>pan</u>-ah-kah."
The underlining shows where to say the word louder. So with Surpanakha, say the "<u>pan</u>" a little louder than the rest.

The MONKEY KING

ONE DAY, THE JADE EMPEROR (who was also chief Chinese God) was playing with a piece of magic stone. He noticed that it looked a little like an animal he knew. So he squeezed it, shaped it, and breathed on it – and there was Sun Hou-tsu (*sun hoo-tzoo*), King of the Monkeys.

Monkey Tricks
In the Middle Ages, someone taking a monkey over Paris's Little Bridge normally had to pay a fee. But if the monkey could perform tricks, it crossed for free.

Monkey God
Not all monkey gods are naughty. Hanuman, the monkey-headed Hindu god, is a brave and faithful friend. He helps Rama rescue Sita from Ravana's stronghold in Sri Lanka (page 23).

Twenty-four hours later, the Emperor realized that he had made a big mistake. Sun was nothing but a troublemaker. He swung from the palace chandeliers and dug up the flowers in the gardens. "It's not fair," Sun complained. "I don't want to be King of the Monkeys. I want to be Ruler of the Universe." The Emperor tried to cheer Sun up by giving him the really important job of Guardian of the Heavenly Peaches. The plan didn't work. When the peaches were laid out for a special banquet of the gods, Sun ate them all.

"That's it!" roared the furious Emperor. "Bring me that moaning monkey!" Sun tried to escape but he was caught in a magic ring and held fast by the Heavenly Dog. When the monkey groveled and begged for mercy, the Emperor stared at him with his hard, jade eyes and shook his head. "Too late!" he snapped. "Take Sun away and strangle him!"

Just then, Buddha, the real Supreme Ruler of the Universe, turned up to ask what all the fuss was about. The Emperor explained. Buddha looked at Sun and asked him why he was such a pain. Sun puffed out his chest and replied, "Because I'm just the Monkey King. I want your job – Supreme Ruler of the Universe. I could do it easily. No sweat."

Buddha thought for a second. "OK," he answered. "You jump somewhere I can't catch you, and you'll be Supreme Ruler of the Universe. Agreed?" "It's a deal!" squeaked Sun. With that, he took a great leap and whooshed through space to the very edge of the universe. There he wrote his name, to prove that he had passed by, before jumping back to Earth again.

"Well, Buddha, you didn't catch me," he boasted. "So now I'm Supreme Ruler of the Universe. Bow to me!" Buddha shook his head. "Not so fast, monkey. Look!" He stretched out his hand and there, on the palm, was written Sun Hou-tsu's name.

Sun stared at his own handwriting for a while then said slowly, "Mmm! I guess being King of the Monkeys is what I'm best at after all, Buddha. Thanks for the lesson. If you let me live I'll keep my big mouth shut from now on… promise!" And he did.

Tail Fin
Most monkeys are great jumpers. When leaping from tree to tree, some monkeys use their tail to keep their balance – a little like the tail fin of an aircraft.

The Real Buddha
Prince Gautama Siddhartha lived in great luxury. But at 29, he saw sickness and death for the first time. He was so upset that he left home to discover the meaning of life. For six years he lived like a poor man. Finally, while he was sitting under a banyan tree, he understood what suffering was about. Now known as the Buddha, he spent the rest of his life passing on his knowledge. The Buddhist religion is based on his teachings.

CHANG LUNG *the* DRAGON

CHANG LUNG WAS ACTING VERY STRANGELY. He did his work and was kind to his wife and nine brawny sons. But his fishing trips were definitely – well – fishy. Whenever possible he went out in his boat alone. Then, instead of returning with his catch, he went to the temple and stayed all night. In the morning, he came home tired, miserable, and soaking wet from the rain.

If his family asked him about his behavior, Chang just muttered some feeble excuse. After a few weeks they had had enough. "Come on, dad," said his eldest son. "It's obvious something's up. What do you do in the temple all night? And why do you always come back looking as if you've spent the night in a field?"

"Do you really want to know?" Chang asked. "Of course we do," replied his son. Chang shrugged. "OK. I look as if I've spent the night in a field because I have. You see, I've become a, er... dragon." "WHA-A-AT?" yelled his family. "Are you kidding? Anyway, where's your tail?"

Chang explained that at the moment he was a dragon only at night. He should be one all the time but an evil dragon had moved into the temple and kicked him out. That's why he got so cold and wet. To get into the temple full-time he had to drive out the evil dragon, but he wasn't strong enough.

Scaly Tale
The legendary emperor Fu-shi (foo-shee) was supposed to have ruled China 5,000 years ago and brought civilization to the country. As the dragon was the symbol of the emperor, Fu-xi was often drawn with a dragon's body.

6

Once his sons got used to the idea of having a fire-breathing dragon dad, they agreed to help. Even his wife came around to the idea. Chang would tie a red ribbon around his neck, become a dragon, and challenge his enemy to a fight. If things went badly, his sons would rescue him by shooting at the dragon without a ribbon.

The next night his sons hid in the shadow of the temple and watched their dad turn himself into a dragon. Shortly afterward, the evil dragon came out into the moonlight. Seeing Chang, he blew fire and pawed the ground with claws like scimitars. Chang backed away. Then, as his enemy reared up to attack, the boys stepped out and fired.

Zap! Zap! Zap! The arrows thudded into the evil beast's neck and body. Roaring horribly, it ran off and died. Chang raised a paw in thanks and slipped into the temple. That's where he's been ever since, watching over his people and sending rain for their crops. So even dragons have their uses – at least the good ones do.

Paper Dragons
In Chinese myth, rain is made by dragons. So if no rain fell, Chinese villagers used to make a huge paper dragon to carry around. If there was still no rain, they tore the paper dragon into pieces to show their anger.

Mystery Bones
Before scientific times, when the Chinese came across dinosaur fossils buried in the ground, they were sure the bones were the remains of dead dragons.

The UGLY SCHOLAR

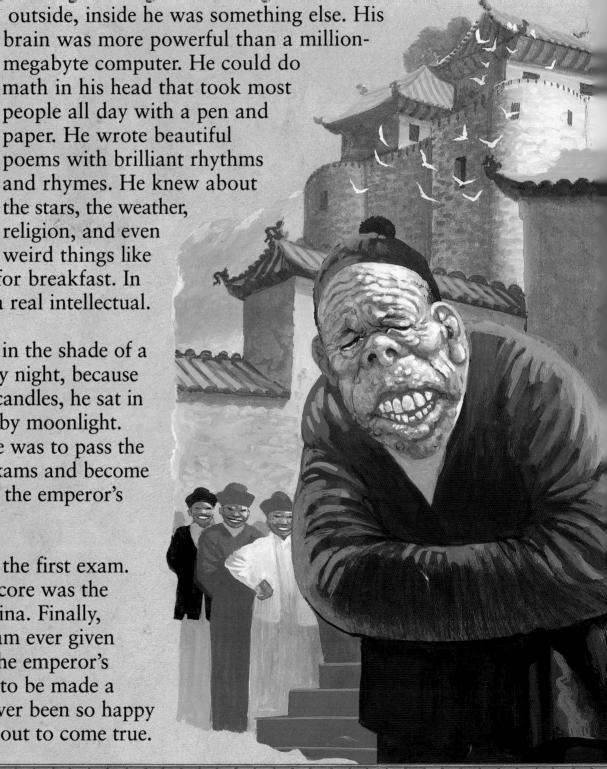

ZHONG KWEI (*chong kway*) was so poor he couldn't afford shoes. All he had to eat was one bowl of rice a day, dished out by a kindly priest. To make matters even worse, he was incredibly ugly. When girls saw him coming, they crossed to the other side of the street. Even dogs ran howling at the sight of his face.

Though Zhong was nothing much on the outside, inside he was something else. His brain was more powerful than a million-megabyte computer. He could do math in his head that took most people all day with a pen and paper. He wrote beautiful poems with brilliant rhythms and rhymes. He knew about the stars, the weather, religion, and even weird things like what dragons had for breakfast. In short, Zhong was a real intellectual.

Top Subjects
Only good students could become "mandarins," officials of the Chinese emperor. They had to study long and difficult books for many years and score high marks in a series of exams.

By day, he studied in the shade of a broad apple tree. By night, because he couldn't afford candles, he sat in the fields and read by moonlight. His only goal in life was to pass the difficult imperial exams and become a mandarin, one of the emperor's top advisors.

He sailed through the first exam. In the second, his score was the highest in all of China. Finally, he passed every exam ever given and was called to the emperor's magnificent palace to be made a mandarin. He'd never been so happy – his dream was about to come true.

But when Zhong's name was called and he stepped forward, a cloud fell over the emperor's face. "Yee-ah-ugh!" he screamed in horror. "Take that hideous, toad-faced THING away from me! How dare anyone suggest that anything so mind-blowingly ugly could be one of my mandarins? Next please!"

The Demon Beater

Chinese families still put up pictures of Zhong Kwei in their home to scare away evil demons. He is often shown holding a demon trap. He uses this to suck in the five creatures that are linked with bad spirits – spiders, snakes, toads, centipedes, and geckos.

Immediately, a pair of guards grabbed Zhong. They marched him out of the palace and flung him into the street. He was shattered. All his long years of work had been pointless. Even the emperor saw only his ugly face, not the intelligence behind it. Sobbing like a child, Zhong wandered out of the city into the countryside. Two days later, he reached the coast, climbed a cliff, and flung himself into the sea.

The gods felt pity for Zhong. A passing sea dragon caught him as he fell through the water and carried him off to heaven. He was placed in his own cluster of stars, the Constellation of Kwei, from where he looks down on the world and judges all writing. He also protects the living from evil demons – a pretty cool thing to do considering how badly other people treated him on Earth.

Bloodsucking Demons

Chinese demons come in all shapes and sizes. Some are like vampires and suck the blood of the living. They have red hair and can only be fought off with weapons of iron or steel.

9

DANCING out the SUN

FOR A LONG TIME Susanowo (*soo-san-no-woe*) and his sister, Amaterasu (*ah-mah-ter-ah-soo*), left each other in peace. He was the Japanese God of the Sea, and he roared about making a storming nuisance of himself. She was the gentle Sun Goddess, smiling on the land and making everyone feel good about themselves.

Things went wrong when windy Susanowo got bored with the sea. He came ashore and began throwing his weight around in Amaterasu's kingdom. He blew down trees and houses and, finally, bit a hole in the roof of his sister's house. His rowdy behavior scared the living daylights out of Amaterasu and she ran away to hide in a cave. Without the Sun Goddess, the world was plunged into darkness.

Who's the Fairest of Them All?
Mirrors have always stood for truth. They cannot lie, as the wicked queen found out when her mirror told her that Snow White was the fairest in the land.

In the endless night, all sorts of demons came out of their holes and made life hell for everyone on Earth. The rest of the gods and goddesses were terrified that their beautiful world was being spoiled, and they begged Amaterasu to come out. When she refused, they piled up jewels in front of the cave and held a party. There was lots of food and great music.

Magical Rocks
Some people believe that jewels have the power to cure or ward off evil. One ancient Chinese princess was covered in precious jade when she died so that her body could live forever.

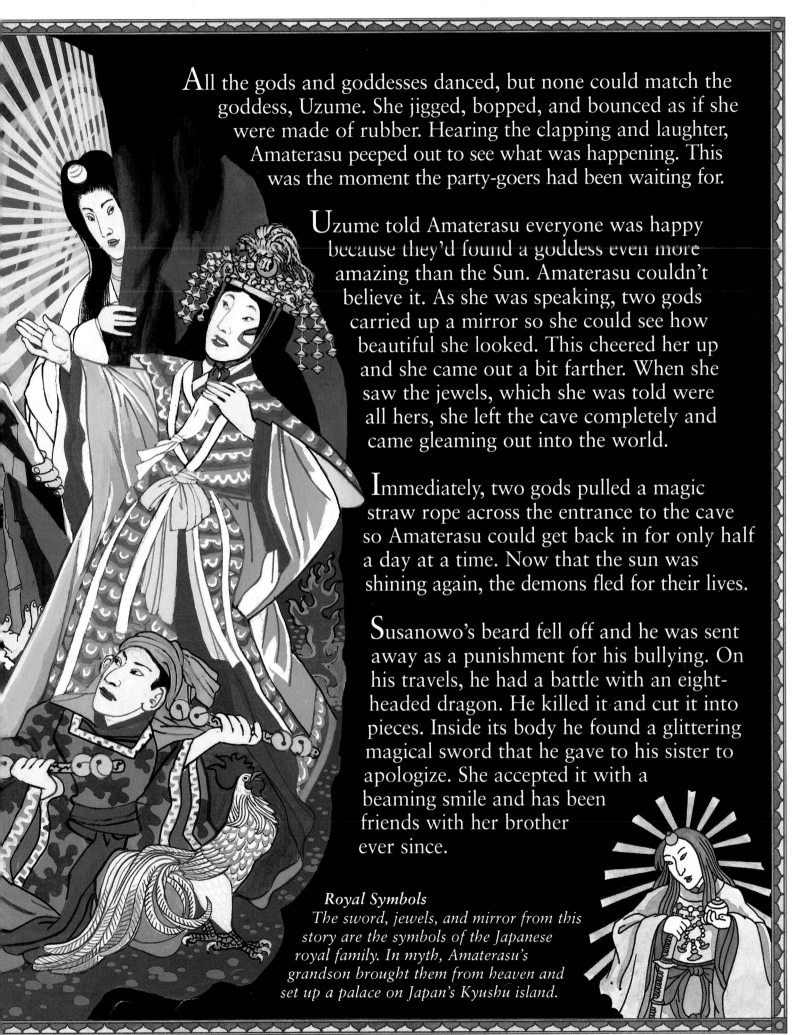

All the gods and goddesses danced, but none could match the goddess, Uzume. She jigged, bopped, and bounced as if she were made of rubber. Hearing the clapping and laughter, Amaterasu peeped out to see what was happening. This was the moment the party-goers had been waiting for.

Uzume told Amaterasu everyone was happy because they'd found a goddess even more amazing than the Sun. Amaterasu couldn't believe it. As she was speaking, two gods carried up a mirror so she could see how beautiful she looked. This cheered her up and she came out a bit farther. When she saw the jewels, which she was told were all hers, she left the cave completely and came gleaming out into the world.

Immediately, two gods pulled a magic straw rope across the entrance to the cave so Amaterasu could get back in for only half a day at a time. Now that the sun was shining again, the demons fled for their lives.

Susanowo's beard fell off and he was sent away as a punishment for his bullying. On his travels, he had a battle with an eight-headed dragon. He killed it and cut it into pieces. Inside its body he found a glittering magical sword that he gave to his sister to apologize. She accepted it with a beaming smile and has been friends with her brother ever since.

Royal Symbols
The sword, jewels, and mirror from this story are the symbols of the Japanese royal family. In myth, Amaterasu's grandson brought them from heaven and set up a palace on Japan's Kyushu island.

The GENERAL and the BEES

THE JAPANESE GENERAL, YOGODAYU (*yo-goh-da-yoo*), got along really well with his sister – until she married. Her husband was mean and greedy, and hated Yogodayu. Before long the two men were arguing, and by the end of the year there was a full-scale war between them.

Things went badly for Yogodayu. His army was ambushed and he only just managed to escape. With only 20 soldiers left, he climbed into the mountains and hid in a cave. Three days later, when his enemies had given up searching for him, he came out to stretch his legs and found a bee stuck in a spider's web. "There you are, little thing," he said, untangling the creature. "You're free to go where you want now. I wish I could say the same for myself."

That night, a man dressed in black and yellow visited Yogodayu in his dreams. The general would win a great victory, he prophesied, if he built a wooden cabin, filled it with empty pots and jars, and let his brother-in-law know where he was.

Bee Post
The ancient Greeks believed bees had something holy about them. They fed Zeus, the King of the Gods, and carried messages for him.

Yogodayu did as he was told. He put together a rough cabin and put inside all the pots he could lay his hands on. Finally, having collected a few more soldiers, he sent a message to his enemy saying he was ready to fight again.

The evil brother-in-law turned up a couple of days later with a huge army. Seeing Yogodayu's tiny band, he burst into laughter. Had he kept quiet, however, and heard the fierce buzzing sound coming from inside the cabin, he might not have thought the situation so funny.

When all was ready, the brother-in-law gave the signal to attack. His men charged forward, yelling wildly. They hadn't gone more than a few steps when a vast black cloud flew out of the cabin and zoomed toward them. It was an enormous swarm of bees! Seconds later they swooped into the attack, stinging Yogodayu's enemies on their arms, legs, and faces.

The army was so busy swatting and dodging, it didn't have time to fight. Yogodayu and his men simply walked up and struck them down by the dozen. In a matter of minutes it was all over. Yogodayu and the bees had triumphed.

The rest of the day was spent gathering up the bees that had been killed. Yogodayu built a temple in their honor and buried them in it with great ceremony. Every year for the rest of his life he worshiped at the bee shrine, thanking his tiny friends for returning one kind deed with another.

One Sting Brings Death
Stinging bees have a poison-injecting spike on their bottom. But it has tiny hooks at the end, so that when the bee flies away, it rips the spike from its body and dies.

The WHITE SERPENT GOD

To the court of the Lord of Gifu came the most skilled swordsmen in Japan. The most brilliant of all was Harada Kurando (*koo-ran-doh*). But he had a rival, Gundayu (*goon-die-yoo*), who believed he was every bit as good as Harada. To see who was better, the Lord of Gifu ordered them to fight. It was a fine contest, but the result was never in doubt. Harada won and was rewarded with a small golden statue of a goddess.

The Emperor's Grasscutter
Japan's most famous sword is the one given by Susanowo to Amaterasu (page 13). It is called Kusangi no Tsurugi, meaning the "grass-cutting sword." It is handed down from emperor to emperor and kept in the Atsutsa Shrine, or Temple of the Sword (above).

Gundayu left the palace in a furious temper, plotting revenge. That night, as Harada was returning home, Gundayu and his gang attacked the champion from behind, killing him and stealing the golden statue. As Gundayu was nowhere to be found, there was little doubt who the murderer was.

The Bushido Boys
The swordsmen in this story were samurai, the knights of Japan. They were skilled fighters and horse riders who followed a code of honor, called the bushido. This code told them to obey their lord, to be brave in battle, and to behave correctly.

The Lord of Gifu gave Yonsuke (*yon-soo-kay*), Harada's son, written permission to avenge his father's death. For five years, he traveled the length and breadth of Japan, seeking the villainous Gundayu. Finally, he tracked him down to a lonely castle in the south. The murderer had taken a false name and was working as a sword master. Not telling anyone who he was, Yonsuke got a job as assistant swordsman to Gundayu.

Shortly afterward, the golden statue disappeared and Yonsuke fell seriously ill. When it was clear he would not live, he asked for a vase of his favorite tree blossom to be placed at his bedside. Two days later, he died. The servant who came to remove the blossom found a small pale snake coiled around the top of the vase and tried to shake it off. The snake held fast.

Nothing would remove the snake until, as a last resort, the servant broke the vase. Out fell the golden statue and a piece of paper. It was the Lord of Gifu's permission for Yonsuke to kill his father's murderer.

Gundayu now realized who his servant had been. When he heard the story of the snake, he was filled with terror at what might happen to him. With good reason, too. He awoke that night to find a white snake coiled tightly around his throat. He let out a horrified cry and tried in vain to pull the creature off. Unmoved, the snake tightened its choking grip and Gundayu died slowly in great agony.

Over the next few days, the full story came out. As a result, the snake was worshiped as the White Serpent God. A shrine was built in its honor, reminding all who went there that whatever they did their sins would always catch up with them.

Beautiful Beginnings
Tree blossom in China and Japan is a beautiful sign of new life and hope for the future after the dark days of winter – just like daffodils are in the United States

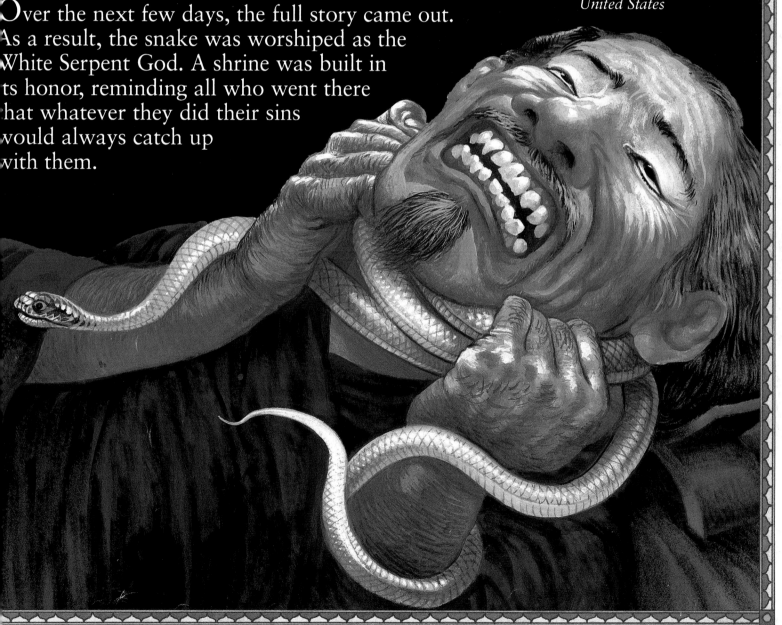

DREAMTIME

BEFORE THERE WAS LIFE ON EARTH, it was Dreamtime. The surface of the world was still, without life, death, plants, animals, birds, or fish. Everything and everyone were asleep. The only living things were the first relatives, who lived deep underground.

The first relatives were an odd-looking bunch, made up of everything that was going to be, all mixed up. Some were human, others were just animals. There were also animals with human parts and humans with animal parts. Bamapama's people were human with missing parts – instead of mouths they had holes in the top of their heads. This made it easy to drink when it rained.

The Role of Rock
The first Australians had no writing. Their culture was passed on by word of mouth or painted on huge rocks, like these figures at Wendjina Rock.

Tube Tunes
The Australians who tell this story have special songmen who play to the people on didgeridoos, long tube instruments that make a deep, eerie noise.

Bamapama lived at the end of Dreamtime, when there were some living things on Earth but no people. In the underground world Bamapama was a real pain, always chasing girls, asking silly questions, and getting into trouble. One day, wandering where he wasn't allowed, he found his way to the surface. Wow! Bamapama had never seen so much space! He ran and jumped around until he caught sight of a kangaroo. It looked good to eat, so he grabbed his spear and went after it. But every time he got close, the kangaroo hopped off and he had to chase it again.

This went on for hours, until it began to get dark. Bamapama had never seen night before because down below it was always daylight. He was petrified. As the shadows crept toward him, he climbed a tree to escape from them. But the higher he climbed, the more the night followed him. In the end, too exhausted to climb any more, he came down and collapsed in a heap on the ground.

When he woke up in the morning – amazing! – it was light again. Bamapama did a little dance to show how happy he was and dashed back underground to tell his family and friends what he had discovered. They didn't believe him at first and they were just as scared as he had been when darkness fell. But they soon got used to night and day and Bamapama's discovery made him a hero.

Bamapama and his people didn't last forever. When real humans came along, the people with holes in the top of their heads changed into the rocks and trees that are all around us today. But be careful! Because they were once our first relatives, they are sacred and full of mystery.

Sacred Stone
To the aboriginal people of Australia the huge pinkish mound, known as Ayers Rock, is sacred to the memory of our first relatives who lived in the Dreamtime.

Big Jumpers
Kangaroos are found only in Australia, Tasmania, and New Guinea. The great gray kangaroo produces one baby (a "joey") a year. It lives in its mother's pouch for about nine months, with odd hops into the outside world.

The VOLCANO GODDESS

THE HAWAIIAN VOLCANO GODDESS PELÉE was hot stuff. It was bad luck for the handsome young Lohiau (*low-hee-ow*), therefore, when she noticed him on the beach she immediately fell for him. She changed herself into a girl so beautiful that no young man, could take his eyes off her. Lohiau fell head over heels in love with her and they were married right away

Pelée's passion burned out as quickly as it had started. After a few weeks, she was bored with Lohiau and went back to being a volcano. He looked everywhere for his lovely wife. When he couldn't find her, his heart broke and he died. This upset Pelée. Although she didn't love Lohiau any more, she still wanted to see him. So, she sent her sister Hiiaka (*hee-yar-kah*) to collect his good-looking remains.

Hiiaka easily found Lohiau's body. But it wasn't much use without his soul, which was held in the soul-prison on a rocky cliff and guarded by two ultra-fierce lizard-women. Hiiaka used all her heavenly skills and courage to outwit the lizard-women and stole Lohiau's soul. Unfortunately, once she'd put it back together with his body and he'd come alive again, she too fell in love with him!

The couple immediately jumped into a canoe and paddled off to Hawaii.

Hot Tempers
As many volcanoes are sacred to the people of the Pacific Ocean, tourists are warned not to take the lava in case they anger a fiery god or goddess.

18

When Pelée saw what was going on, she was angry, jealous, and upset. She showed her emotions in the most spectacular way she could – by erupting. Hiiaka was used to her sister's tricks and escaped, but poor Lohiau was covered in molten lava and died a second time.

Floating Art
The canoes of the people of the Pacific are not just a way of getting around. Some are floating works of art, carved and painted with wonderful skill.

At this point the Father of the Gods, who had a soft spot for Hiiaka, decided Pelée had gone too far. Taking pity on Lohiau, he dug him out of his lava coffin, stuck together his body and soul, and brought him back into a third life. The god then had a talk with Pelée. Not even a volcano, he pointed out, should stand in the way of true love. Pelée agreed and told the confused Lohiau where he could find his beloved Hiiaka.

She was taking part in an All-Pacific Song Contest. Lohiau turned up as she was starting a song about how handsome and kind he was. When she got to the second verse, he joined in and sang of her beauty. Recognizing his voice, she rushed into his arms and they sailed off into the sunset for a life of happiness.

Lava Coffins
Mount Vesuvius erupted in A.D. 79 and covered the Roman town of Pompeii in ash and lava. Some 1,900 years later, historians poured plaster into holes in the lava to show the outline of the victims' bodies.

The DOLPHIN MOTHER

"ONE BED – GOOD. Two mats – that's right. Four cups, four plates, a knife…" Sukato did this every morning and evening. He counted all his furniture, all his cutlery and, of course, all his money. Nothing in the house could be bought, sold, or eaten without his permission. He was without doubt the meanest miser on all the island of Java, in Indonesia.

Beast or Beauty?
Some people think the mermaid myth comes from mistaking the identity of the quaint-looking dugong, a kind of sea mammal. The mistake is just possible – but you'd have to be at a distance, in the dark, and without your glasses!

One day, while Sukato was out looking for coins that people had dropped in the street, his three children came in from the fields and asked their mother, Tela, for something to eat. "No, my dears," she sighed. "I cannot give you anything without your father's permission." "Please, Mom," begged the kids. "We're starving!"

Tela's heart almost broke when she looked at her thin, ragged children and thought of the food piled up in the store. In the end she agreed to give them just one little dried fish each. They thanked her, wolfed them down, and ran out to play again.

Sukato came back late that afternoon. Having locked away the three coins he'd found, he began his nightly check. Tela busied herself with making dinner, trying not to show how scared she was. By the time he got to the dried fish, she was almost sick with worry. "77, 78, 79… " he counted. Then he stopped and began again.

Family Matters
Dolphins are highly intelligent creatures that like to live together. They carefully guard their young and have even been known to help human swimmers who get into trouble.

When he got to 79 a second time, he called to Tela, "Wife, there are three fish missing! Where are they?" "Please don't be mad," she pleaded. "I gave them to the children. They were so hungry!" "What!" screamed Sukato. "You gave away my food to those greedy pigs! How dare you!" He went purple with rage, and began waving his fists and screaming at his wife.

Fishy Tales
To explain why ships sometimes ran into rocks for no obvious reason, sailors used to say that they had been lured there by sexy-looking mermaids.

Tela feared for her life. With tears streaming down her face, she ran down to the sea to wash herself. Amazingly, as the water lapped against her legs, from the waist down she turned into a dolphin. When the children came looking for her and saw what had happened, they too began to cry. "Don't weep, dear children," she said. "The sea is my home now. But take my tears and rub them into your father's back when he's asleep and he'll realize the terrible things he has done."

The children did as their mother asked. The next morning Sukato was filled with shame for his meanness and cruelty, and he hurried down to the shore to look for his wife. He never found her, but the dolphin's sad cry can still be heard to this day.

RAMA *and* SITA

RAMA THE DEMI-GOD was born in mystery. He grew up a noble young man, tall, good-looking, and extremely strong. His bravery was soon a legend – there wasn't a village in all of India that didn't know how he had killed the terrible demoness, Taraka.

Air Travel
Rama is the human form of the Hindu god, Vishnu. Vishnu, the restorer, travels around on the back of Garuda, the Sun bird and enemy of all serpents.

It wasn't easy finding a wife for such a hero. The most suitable was the lovely Sita, daughter of King Janaka. The king wanted a really special husband for her, so he said she could marry whoever could bend his ancient bow. Inspired by Sita's beauty, many men tried and failed. But when Rama tried, he not only bent the bow but pulled it so far it broke! So Rama and Sita were married and grew very close.

By now Rama was a powerful king, hated by the forces of evil. Among his enemies was a wicked aunt who plotted against the royal couple and got them banished into the gloomy forest. Here lurked demons as wicked as sin. One of them, the sinister Surpanakha (*sir-pan-ah-kah*), took a liking to Rama and asked him to run off with her. Madly in love with his beautiful wife, Rama would have nothing to do with her.

Mighty Bow Benders
The story of Rama and Sita is found in the ancient Indian poem, the Ramayana. The tale of Rama bending a bow to win the hand of Sita is like the Greek myth of Odysseus, who bent a mighty bow to win back his wife, Penelope.

Surpanakha's brother, the ten-headed demon Ravana, was furious that Rama had rejected his sister. In revenge, he seized Sita with his 20 arms and carried her off to his island kingdom in Sri Lanka. Rama now faced the greatest challenge of his life. He collected an army, including a force of brave warrior monkeys, and set out to rescue his captive wife.

Demon Enemies
Rama's monkey army was led by Hanuman, the monkey god. In the battle against the demons, they had to fight the rakshasas, ugly spirits that can fly faster than the wind.

Helped by the King of the Ocean, Rama's army crossed from southern India to Sri Lanka. The battle of demons, monkeys, and men was long and furious until Rama pierced Ravana's iron heart with a flaming weapon given to him by the gods. Sita, glorious in her beauty, now came to Rama and the two were once again united.

Over the years, however, people spread rumors about Sita. Perhaps she wasn't as pure as everyone said? Maybe she'd been happy to go off with Ravana? Rama heard these stories and was troubled. He told them to Sita, who wept and asked Mother Earth to prove her innocence. All at once, the earth opened and a golden throne appeared. Sita climbed onto it, the earth closed, and she disappeared from view.

Rama, now certain of Sita's innocence, was in an agony of sorrow. He could not live without her. The Heavenly Bird, hearing his sobbing, flew down and carried him off to be with his beloved Sita forever.

DEADLY RIVALRY

LONG AGO, the beautiful Pritha and Indra, the Sun King, had a son named Karna. But Pritha was ashamed of her child and got rid of him by floating him down India's Ganges River in a basket. She then married a king and had many valiant sons, known as the Pandavas. Unknown to her, Karna grew into a great warrior, with lion eyes, the shoulders of a bull, and a gleaming suit of golden armor.

Sitting Comfortably?
The story of Karna and Arjuna is told in the holy and ancient Hindu poem, the Mahabharata. This long story, crammed full of amazing adventures, takes days to tell in full.

When Pritha's royal husband died, his blind brother took over the throne. His queen always wore a blindfold so she could not see either. Like Pritha, she too had lots of soldier sons. These were the Kauravas. Not surprisingly, the Pandavas and their cousins the Kauravas were great rivals. Each gang believed it was braver and more skilled than the other.

So they could show off their talents, the king arranged a fantastic tournament. There had never been anything like it. Brilliant flags and banners fluttered in the breeze. Bright jewels and bowls of scented flowers decorated miles of tents, golden pavilions, and masts.

Hundreds of thousands of spectators poured into the stands to watch. They saw archers shoot skillfully from the backs of elephants, furious chariot racing, and mock fighting that at times got dangerously close to the real thing. But the real star of the tournament was the glittering Arjuna, the leader of the Pandavas.

Arjuna rode fastest, shot farthest, and straightest, and could overcome anyone with his sword or spear. His success made the Kauravas extremely jealous. Then, just as the tournament was ending, the magnificent Karna turned up. His mother recognized him at once, but didn't dare tell anyone who he was.

Karna turned out to be just as talented as Arjuna. Although they didn't know of his holy birth, the Kauravas made him their champion against Arjuna. Now the crowd wanted to know who was the better warrior. The only way to find out was for them to fight. However, at the last minute the battle was canceled because no one knew where Karna had come from. Only the queen knew that he and Arjuna were brothers.

By now the spectators were crazy about Karna. Believing he must have had royal parents, they chose him as their king and crowned him with great ceremony. But the rejoicing did not last. The rivalry between the Kauravas and Pandavas soon turned into war. Both Karna and Arjuna were killed. The struggle, full of slaughter, magic, mystery, and murder, lasted for years until Indra, the Sun King, brought peace at last.

The Love God
Another set of great Hindu stories are the Puranas. One of the main characters in these tales is Krishna, another form of the god Vishnu. He is a passionate lover who is popular with women.

The ELEPHANT GOD

THE GODDESS PARVATI felt dirty. She wasn't dirty, she just felt that way and, being the daughter of the Indian Mountain King, she was allowed to feel how she wanted. What she really wanted was a long, hot bath in peace, but this was going to be a bit tricky.

Elephants Never Forget
From the earliest times people have believed elephants to be intelligent and blessed with excellent memories. Aristotle, the ancient Greek philosopher, said they were the cleverest animals of all.

The problem was her husband, Siva the Terrible One. He looked pleasant enough (if you didn't mind his four arms, four faces, and three eyes), but he had a ferocious temper. Once, when the love god Karma disturbed his meditation, he burned him up with a flash of lightning from his middle eye. So there was no point in asking Siva to keep out of the bathroom. He had to be kept out.

When her bath was steaming hot and bubbly, Parvati asked her chubby son, Ganesa, to guard the door and climbed in for a good soak. As luck would have it, at this moment Siva rode up. He tied up his trusty steed (a milk-white bull) and came into the house. Seeing clouds of steam coming from the bathroom, he went to see what was going on. Ganesa blocked his way. "Sorry, dad," he smiled, "but mom's having a bath and wants to be left in peace." Siva was not amused.

Using Their Loaf
Ganesa is the Hindu god of wisdom and good luck. He rides on another wise animal – the rat. The ancient Egyptians believed rats were wise because they always ate the best bread.

"Get out of my way, boy," Siva ordered. Ganesa didn't move. The god's temper flared like fire. With one movement he seized a sword, sliced off Ganesa's head and kicked it into orbit. "Hello? Who's there?" called Parvati from the other side of the door.

Siva froze. What had he done? "Er, it's me. Siva. I'm afraid we've had a terrible accident." There was a splashing noise, then the door opened and Parvati appeared, wrapped in a towel. "What… ?" she gasped when she saw the headless body of her son. Siva shuffled his feet and looked embarrassed. "Mend him at once!" Parvati cried, pulling herself together.

There was no way Siva could get Ganesa's head back, so he went outside to look for a substitute. Seeing a passing elephant, he cut off its head and ran back inside. "Ready, sweetheart," he called a couple of seconds later. There was more splashing and once again Parvati opened the door.

There stood her son, full of life but with an elephant's head instead of a human one. The goddess was furious at first but soon calmed down. Ganesa didn't mind his new head, either. He found it full of wisdom, which earned him the respect of professors and all kinds of intellectuals.

Tusk Master
Ganesa is supposed to have written the Mahabharata with some of his tusk that Rama had chopped off. Because he is such a good writer, Ganesa often appears at the front of Indian students' school books.

TRICKY TERMS

Words in italics, e.g. *souls*, have their own explanation.

Buddhist
Someone who believes in the teachings of Buddha, an Indian prince born in 563 B.C. The Buddhist religion started in northeast India, then spread to China, Tibet, Thailand, Myanmar, and Vietnam.

Demon
An evil *spirit* that fights against the forces of good.

Heaven
The home of gods and the *souls* of people who have led good lives. Some Eastern religions believe that advanced believers can pass heaven and reach an eternal state, known as Nirvana.

Hindu
Most Hindus live in India. They do not always share the same ideas, but most believe in the supreme god, Brahman. Other Hindu gods, such as Vishnu the Preserver and Siva the Destroyer, show different parts of Brahman's nature.

Immortal
A living thing that can never die or be killed.

Legend
A story that has grown up around a person or an event, which may have taken place.

Ritual
A set of holy actions that form part of religious worship. Many big events in our lives, such as birth, marriage, and death, are marked by rituals.

Sacred
The most important parts of religion, or anything holy.

Shinto
Shinto is the oldest religion in Japan and is closely linked to Buddhism. The word Shinto means "way of the gods." Unlike Western religions, there is no organized church. Instead, Shinto believers visit shrines honoring gods, local *spirits*, and the royal family.

Soul
The part of a creature that thinks and feels. Some peoples believe that a soul is *immortal*, and that when a person or creature dies, their soul goes to *heaven*.

Spirit
A living being that has no body. Spirit can also mean the *soul* of a creature.

Taoist and Confucianist
The Chinese have traditionally followed the teachings of three men: *Buddha*, Confucius, and Lao Zi. Confucius taught about respecting your parents and the old. Lao Zi, founder of Taoism, taught about living your life according to the laws of nature.

The Chinese Horoscope (*center of page*)
In Chinese myth, Buddha once invited all the animals in the world to visit him. But only 12 showed up. To thank them, he named a year after each one. To this day, many people believe that if you are born in a particular animal's year, you will inherit some of its character. If you were born in one of these 12 years, see what animal you are linked to:

Tiger (*brave*)	February 9, 1986 – January 28, 1987	Monkey (*helpful*)	February 4, 1992 – January 22, 1993
Rabbit (*quiet*)	January 29, 1987 – February 16, 1988	Rooster (*lively*)	January 23, 1993 – February 9, 1994
Dragon (*confident*)	February 17, 1988 – February 5, 1989	Dog (*loyal*)	February 10, 1994 – January 30, 1995
Snake (*wise*)	February 6, 1989 – January 26, 1990	Pig (*honest*)	January 31, 1995 – February 18, 1996
Horse (*charming*)	January 27, 1990 – February 14, 1991	Rat (*friendly*)	February 19, 1996 – February 6, 1997
Goat (*artistic*)	February 15, 1991 – February 3, 1992	Ox (*hard-working*)	February 7, 1997 – January 27, 1998

WHO'S WHO

A guide to the greatest names in Asian and Pacific myth and legend. Names in capitals, e.g. IZANAGI, have their own explanation.

Amaterasu (*ah-mah-ter-ah-soo*)
The Sun Goddess in Shinto mythology, who was born from the left eye of IZANAGI.

Amrita (*um-ree-tuh*)
The Hindu Water of Eternal Life. The gods produced Amrita by churning up the Ocean of Milk. They used a mountain turned by a thousand-headed serpent. The god VISHNU took the form of a turtle so his shell would give something for the mountain to spin on.

But, demons grabbed the amrita after it had been made. If they had drunk it, they would have become far stronger than the gods. So, Vishnu became a beautiful woman. The demons began arguing over her and in the meantime Vishnu stole back the amrita for the gods.

Azure Dragon
There are many dragons in Chinese mythology. One of the most famous is the Azure (blue) Dragon, the spirit of a 14th-century Chinese hero who had fought against evil spirits.

Baime (*by-may*)
A creator god in Australian myths. He is said to have created the rivers, hills, and trees of Australia.

Brahma (*bra-mah*)
The Hindu Creator God of the Universe. In one story, he is born from a golden egg that floated on the first waters. Brahma is usually shown with four faces and wearing a white robe.

Devi (*deh-vee*)
The Hindu Mother Goddess. She can appear in many different forms, and is often shown as Siva's wife. Sometimes, when she appears, she is the kind and gentle goddess, Lakshmi. But she can also be the powerful and destructive Kali (*page 30*).

Ayers Rock

Ganesa (*gun-nair-sha*)
The elephant-headed Hindu God of Wisdom. Hindus feed Ganesa's hungry pot-bellied stomach with large offerings of fruit and vegetables.

Guan Di (*gwan dee*)
The Chinese God of War. In one tale, he rescued a young woman who had been put in jail by an evil official. When he hid in a temple to avoid capture, soldiers set fire to the building. Guan Di leapt out and killed them all. But the flames had turned his face bright red – which is why he is always shown with a red face.

Guan Yin (*gwan yeen*)
The Chinese Goddess of Mercy and Protector of Children. In myth, she was the daughter of a wicked ruler. When she asked to become a Buddhist nun, her father had her killed.

Her soul went to hell, but it was so saintly that it turned hell into a paradise. The gods were so worried by this that they asked Buddha to bring Guan Yin back to life and restore the hell to its horrible old ways.

Io
The all-powerful god in the myths of the Maori people of New Zealand.

29

Ganesa

Izanagi and Izanami (*iz-an-nah-gee* and *iz-an-nah-mee*)
Izanagi and Izanami, created the Japanese islands, and gave birth to many gods and goddesses, including AMATERASU.

Kadaklan (*ka-dack-lan*)
A creator god from the myths of the Philippine Islands in the Pacific. He bangs on his drum to make thunder, and lightning is caused by his dog barking.

Lac Long Quan
(*lack long kwan*)
A dragon lord from Vietnam mythology, who taught his people how to farm rice and make clothes.

Maui (*mah-oo-ee*)
In Polynesian myth, Maui fished up their islands from the bottom of the Pacific Ocean using a giant hook (*right*). He also caught the sun in a giant lasso to slow it down as it sped across the sky. He did this so that people would have more time during the day to cook their meals.

Nats
The name for supernatural spirits in Myanmar that can be good or evil.

O Kuni Nushi
(*oh koo-nee noo-shee*)
The Shinto God of Medicine, who fell in love with Susanowo's daughter then married her. Susanowo was so angry he tried to kill O Kuni Nushi by putting snakes and poisonous insects into his bed, but O Kuni Nushi escaped using a magic scarf.

Olofat (*oh-loh-fat*)
A trickster god who brought fire to the people of Micronesia in the Pacific.

Pan Ku
(*pan koo*)
The Creator of the Universe in Chinese myths. At the beginning of time, all that existed was a giant egg, which contained chaos and the huge Pan Ku. When Pan Ku broke out of the egg, chaos also escaped. The lighter, purer parts, known as Yang, floated up to become the sky. The heavier parts, known as Yin, sank to become the earth. For 18,000 years, Pan Ku keep the Yin and the Yang apart, until the sky was fixed above the earth. Then he died, and from his body were made the sun, moon, and stars.

Kali

Pelée (*pel-lay*)
The Hawaiian Volcano Goddess. When her husband ran away, Pelée wept so much that her tears covered all but the highest mountains of Hawaii, leaving the islands surrounded by sea.

Rangda (*rang-dah*)
An evil she-demon in the myths of Bali in Indonesia.

Siva (_shee-vah_)

Along with BRAHMA and VISHNU, Siva the Destroyer is one of the three major Hindu gods. In one story, Siva's hair divided the waters of the Ganges River as it fell to the earth, forming seven holy rivers.

Tsao Wang (_tsow wang_)

The Chinese Kitchen God watches families from above the hearth. At the end of each year, he reports back to the Jade Emperor on their behavior. The day before, a family will spread honey on his lips so that he only speaks sweet words.

Tengu (_ten-goo_)

These naughty spirits are from Japan. Their name means "long nose," because they are half-human and half-bird, with wings, claws, and long beaks.

Urashima

Tsuki Yomi (_tsooki yoh-mee_)

This Shinto Moon God was born from the right eye of IZANAGI. He climbed up the Ladder of Heaven to live with his sister, AMATERASU.

But when he killed the Goddess of Food, his sister refused to see him again, which is why the sun and moon always appear at different times.

Urashima (_oo-rah-shee-mah_)

A shrine on the Japanese island of Tango is dedicated to the memory of a local fisherboy, Urashima, who married a mermaid. He went to live in her undersea palace, but after a while he really wanted to see his parents once more.

The mermaid gave Urashima a box that would allow him to return home – as long as it remained closed. Finding he had been away for hundreds of years, the boy opened the box and instantly shriveled into a skeleton.

Varuna (_var-roo-nah_)

A Hindu sky god who knows everything there is to know because he has a thousand eyes that can see all things. In one myth, Varuna travels on the back of Makara, a beast that is part-dolphin, part-shark, and part-crocodile.

Vishnu (_vish-noo_)

One of the three great Hindu gods, Vishnu the Protector comes to Earth when it is in trouble to sort things out. To do this, he takes on human form, such as Rama.

Varuna

Walwalag Sisters

These sisters are Australian sky beings. In one myth, on their travels they upset the Great Rainbow Snake, YURLUNGGUR, by dirtying its waterhole. Though the sisters sang and danced, the snake swallowed them. The snake later vomited up the sisters, and green ants bit them and restored them to life.

Weretigers (_below left_)

In Malaysia, the tiger was known as "stripey face." According to one myth, if you mentioned its name you called a weretiger. They were the souls of the dead that could change into vicious tigers. There were also weretigers in the myths of Java, but these were friendly creatures.

Yurlunggur (_yer-lung-gerr_)

One of the many names for the Australian Great Rainbow Snake, which like other sky beings, was a creator of the landscape, especially waterholes and rivers. In some myths, the snake caused a great flood that washed away the world that existed before this one.

31

INDEX

*The main stories for each name have page numbers in **bold**.*

Amaterasu **10–11**, 14, 29, 30, 31
Amrita 29
Arjuna 24–25

Baime 29
Bamapama 16–17
Brahma **29**, 31
Brahman 28
Buddha 4, **5**, 29
Buddhists 5, **28**

Chung Lung 3, **6–7**
Confucius 28

Demons **9**, 10, 11, 22, 23
Devi 29
Dolphin Mother 3, **20–21**
Dragons 3, 6–7, **8–9**, 11, 29
Dreamtime 3, **16–17**

Father of the Gods 19
First relatives 16–17
Fu-shi 6

Ganesa **26–27**, 29
Garuda 22
General Yogodayu 12–13

Guan Di 29
Guan Yin 29
Gundayo 14–15

Hanuman 4, 23
Harada Kurando 14

Hiiaka 18, 19
Hindus 4, 22, 24, 25, 27, **28**

Indra 25
Io 29
Izanagi 29, **30**, 31
Izanami 30

Jade Emperor 4

Kadaklan 30
Kali **29**, 30
Karma 26
Karna 24–25
King Janaka 22
Krishna 25
Kusangi no Tsuragi 14

Lac Long Quan 30
Lakshmi 29
Lao Zi 28
Lohiau 18–19
Lord of Gifu 14, 15

Mahabharata 24, 27
Maui 30
Monkey King 4–5
Mother Earth 23
Mountain King 26

Nats 30

Odysseus 22
O Kuni Nushi 30
Olofat 30

Pan Ku 30
Parvati 26–27
Pelée **18–19**, 30
Pritha 24

Rakshasas 23
Rama 3, 4, **22–23**, 27, 31

Ramayana 22
Rangda 30
Ravana 4, **23**
Ruler of the Universe 4

Shinto **28**, 29, 30
Sita 3, 4, **22–23**
Siva 26, 27, 28, 31
Sukato 20, 21
Surpanakha 3, 22, 23
Susanowo 10–11, 14

Taoism 28
Taraka 22
Tela 21
Tengu 31
Tsao Wang 31
Tsuki Yomi 31

Urashima 31
Uzume 11

Varuna 31
Vishnu 22, 25, 28, 29, 31

Walwalag Sisters 31
Weretigers 31

Yonsuke 14, 15
Yurlunggur 31

Zhong Kwei 8–9